Collins

Maths Progress Tests for White Rose

Year 1/P2

Cherri Moseley

William Collins' dream of knowledge for all began with the publication of his first book in 1819. A self-educated mill worker, he not only enriched millions of lives, but also founded a flourishing publishing house. Today, staying true to this spirit, Collins books are packed with inspiration,
innovation and practical expertise. They place you at the centre of a world of possibility and give you exactly what you need to explore it.

Collins. Freedom to teach.

Collins
An imprint of HarperCollins*Publishers*
The News Building
1 London Bridge Street
London
SE1 9GF

MIX
Paper from
responsible sources

FSC™ C007454

This book is produced from independently certified FSC™ paper to ensure responsible forest management.

For more information visit: **www.harpercollins.co.uk/green**

Browse the complete Collins catalogue at
www.collins.co.uk

© HarperCollinsPublishers Limited 2019

10 9 8 7 6 5 4 3 2 1

ISBN 978-0-00-833349-2

British Library Cataloguing in Publication Data. A catalogue record for this publication is available from the British Library.

Author: Cherri Moseley
Publisher: Katie Sergeant
Commissioning Editor: Fiona Lazenby
Product Developer: Mike Appleton
Copyeditor: Joan Miller
Proofreader: Catherine Dakin
Design and Typesetting: Ken Vail Graphic Design
Cover Design: The Big Mountain Design
Production controller: Katharine Willard
Printed and bound by CPI Group (UK) Ltd, Croydon, CR0 4YY

Contents

How to use this book

Introduction

Collins Maths Progress Tests for White Rose have been designed to give you a consistent whole-school approach to teaching and assessing mathematics. Each photocopiable book covers the required mathematics objectives from the 2014 Primary English National Curriculum. For teachers in Scotland, the books can offer guidance and structure that is not provided in the Curriculum for Excellence Experiences and Outcomes or Benchmarks for Numeracy and Mathematics.

As stand-alone tests, the *Collins Maths Progress Tests for White Rose* provide a structured way to assess progress in arithmetic and reasoning skills, to help you identify areas for development, and to provide evidence towards expectations for each year group. Whilst the tests are independent of any textbook-based teaching and learning scheme to allow for maximum flexibility, the content for each test has been selected based on the suggested teaching order in the *White Rose Maths Schemes of Learning*, which are designed to support a mastery approach to teaching and learning.

Assessment of mathematical skills

At the end of KS1 and KS2, children sit tests to assess the standards they have reached in mathematics. This is done through national curriculum tests (SATs) in Arithmetic and Mathematical Reasoning. *Collins Maths Progress Tests for White Rose* have been designed to provide children with opportunities to explore a range of question types whilst building familiarity with the format, language and style of the SATs.

The Arithmetic tests comprise constructed response questions, presented as context-free calculations, to assess pupils' confidence with a range of mathematics operations as appropriate to the year group. Questions come from the Number, Ratio and Algebra domains.

The Reasoning tests present mathematical problems in a wide range of formats to ensure pupils can fully demonstrate mathematical fluency, mathematical problem solving and mathematical reasoning. They include both selected response questions (e.g. multiple choice, matching, yes/no) and constructed response questions. Questions may draw on all content domains and approximately half of the questions in the Reasoning tests are presented in context.

The tests follow the structure and format of SATs mathematics papers and are pitched at a level appropriate to age-related expectations for the year group. They provide increasing challenge within each year group and across the school, both in terms of content and cognitive demand, but also with increasing numbers of questions to build stamina and resilience. Using the progress tests with your classes at the end of

each half-term should help pupils to develop and practise the necessary skills required to complete the national tests with confidence, as well as offering you a snapshot of their progress at those points throughout the year. You can use the results formatively to help identify gaps in knowledge and next teaching steps.

How to use this book

In this book, you will find twelve photocopiable tests: one arithmetic test and one reasoning test for use at the end of each half term of teaching. Each child will need a copy of the test. You will find Curriculum Content Coverage on page vi indicating the White Rose Scheme of Learning Block and associated Content Domain topics covered in each test across the year group. The specific Content Domain references indicating the year, strand and substrand, e.g. 2N1, for the questions in each test are in the tables on page 95. You may find it useful to make a photocopy of these tables for each child and highlight questions answered incorrectly to help identify any consistent areas of difficulty.

The number of marks available and suggested timing to be allowed are indicated for each test. The number of marks/questions in each test and the length of time allowed increases gradually across the year as summarised in the table below. Note that the Year 2 and Year 6 Summer term tests have been written as full practice papers assuming that all content will have been taught by this point. They mirror the number of marks and time allowed in the end of Key Stage 1 and end of Key Stage 2 test papers.

Year group	Test	Time allowed	Number of marks
1	Autumn 1 Arithmetic	10 minutes	10
1	Autumn 1 Reasoning	18 minutes	15
1	Autumn 2 Arithmetic	10 minutes	10
1	Autumn 2 Reasoning	18 minutes	15
1	Spring 1 Arithmetic	15 minutes	12
1	Spring 1 Reasoning	22 minutes	18
1	Spring 2 Arithmetic	15 minutes	12
1	Spring 2 Reasoning	22 minutes	18
1	Summer 1 Arithmetic	18 minutes	15
1	Summer 1 Reasoning	24 minutes	20
1	Summer 2 Arithmetic	18 minutes	15
1	Summer 2 Reasoning	24 minutes	20

To help you mark the tests, you will find mark schemes at the back of the book. These include the answer requirement, number of marks to be awarded, additional guidance on answers that should or should not be accepted and when to award marks for working in multi-mark questions.

Test demand

The tests have been written to assess progress in children's arithmetic and mathematical reasoning skills with the content and cognitive demand of questions increasing within each book and across the series to build towards to end of key stage expectations of the SATs. Since the national tests may cover content from the whole key stage, each progress test contains some questions which draw on content from earlier terms or previous year objectives (particularly in autumn term tests). This ensures that prior content and skills are revisited.

The level of demand for each question has been provided within the mark schemes for each test using the notation T (working towards), E (expected standard) or G (greater depth). These ratings are given as an indication of the level of complexity of each question taking into account the thinking skills required to understand what is being asked, the computational complexity in calculating the answer, spatial reasoning or data interpretation required and the response strategy for the question.

Performance thresholds

The table below provides guidance for assessing how children perform in the tests. Most children should achieve scores at or above the expected standard, with some children working at greater depth and exceeding expectations for their year group. While the thresholds bands do not represent standardised scores, as in the end of key stage SATs, they will give an indication of how pupils are performing against the expected standards for their year group. The thresholds have been set broadly assuming that pupils who achieve greater than 60% will be working at the expected standard and those who

score more than 80% are likely to be working at greater depth. However, pupils will all have individual strengths and weaknesses, so it is possible that they could be working towards the expected standard in some areas but at greater depth in others. For this reason, using the content domain coverage tables to identify common areas of difficulty alongside your own professional judgement, will enable you to identify pupils' specific gaps in knowledge and areas where further teaching may be required.

Tracking progress

A record sheet is provided to help you illustrate to children the areas in which their arithmetic and reasoning skills are strong and where they need to develop. A spreadsheet tracker is also provided via collins.co.uk/assessment/downloads which enables you to identify whole-class patterns of attainment. This can be used to inform your next teaching and learning steps.

Editable download

All the files are available online in Word and PDF format. Go to collins.co.uk/assessment/downloads to find instructions on how to download. The files are password protected and the password clue is included on the website. You will need to use the clue to locate the password in your book.

You can use these editable files to help you meet the specific needs of your class, whether that be by increasing or decreasing the challenge, by reducing the number of questions, by providing more space for answers or increasing the size of text for specific children.

Year group	Test	Working towards (T)	Expected standard (E)	Greater depth (G)
1	Autumn 1 Arithmetic	5 marks or below	6–7 marks	8–10 marks
1	Autumn 1 Reasoning	8 marks or below	9–11 marks	12–15 marks
1	Autumn 2 Arithmetic	5 marks or below	6–7 marks	8–10 marks
1	Autumn 2 Reasoning	8 marks or below	9–11 marks	12–15 marks
1	Spring 1 Arithmetic	6 marks or below	7–9 marks	10–12 marks
1	Spring 1 Reasoning	9 marks or below	10–14 marks	15–18 marks
1	Spring 2 Arithmetic	6 marks or below	7–9 marks	10–12 marks
1	Spring 2 Reasoning	9 marks or below	10–14 marks	15–18 marks
1	Summer 1 Arithmetic	8 marks or below	9–11 marks	12–15 marks
1	Summer 1 Reasoning	11 marks or below	12–15 marks	16–20 marks
1	Summer 2 Arithmetic	8 marks or below	9–11 marks	12–15 marks
1	Summer 2 Reasoning	11 marks or below	12–15 marks	16–20 marks

Curriculum content coverage

All content objectives from the Year 1 National Curriculum Programme of Study for Mathematics are covered within one or more of the half-termly progress tests across the year. The content for each test is based on the suggested teaching order of the White Rose Maths Schemes of Learning. The table below shows from which teaching blocks the content for each test is drawn. Where the White Rose Maths blocks are devoted to skills or consolidation rather than introduction of new content, these blocks are not covered by the tests. The Summer tests for Year 1 draw on content from previous blocks.

White Rose Schemes of Learning blocks			Collins Maths Progress Tests for White Rose											
Blocks	Weeks	Topics	Autumn 1: Arithmetic	Autumn 1: Reasoning	Autumn 2: Arithmetic	Autumn 2: Reasoning	Spring 1: Arithmetic	Spring 1: Reasoning	Spring 2: Arithmetic	Spring 2: Reasoning	Summer 1: Arithmetic	Summer 1: Reasoning	Summer 2: Arithmetic	Summer 2: Reasoning
Autumn Block 1	Weeks 1–4	Number: Place Value (within 10)	✔	✔							✔	✔	✔	✔
Autumn Block 2	Weeks 5–8	Number: Addition and Subtraction (within 10)	✔	✔	✔	✔					✔	✔	✔	✔
Autumn Block 3	Week 9	Geometry: Shape				✔						✔		✔
Autumn Block 4	Weeks 10–11	Number: Place Value (within 20)			✔	✔					✔	✔		✔
Autumn Block 5	Week 12	Consolidation												
Spring Block 1	Weeks 1–4	Number: Addition and Subtraction (within 20)					✔	✔			✔	✔	✔	✔
Spring Block 2	Weeks 5–7	Number: Place Value (within 50) (Multiples of 2, 5, and 10 to be included)					✔	✔	✔	✔	✔	✔	✔	✔
Spring Block 3	Weeks 8–9	Measurement: Length and Height								✔		✔	✔	✔
Spring Block 4	Weeks 10–11	Measurement: Weight and Volume								✔		✔		✔
Spring Block 5	Week 12	Consolidation												
Summer Block 1	Weeks 1–3	Number: Multiplication and Division (Reinforce multiples of 2, 5 and 10 to be included)									✔	✔	✔	✔
Summer Block 2	Weeks 4-5	Number: Fractions									✔	✔	✔	✔
Summer Block 3	Week 6	Geometry: Position and Direction										✔		✔
Summer Block 4	Weeks 7–8	Number: Place Value (within 100)											✔	✔
Summer Block 5	Week 9	Measurement: Money												✔
Summer Block 6	Weeks 10–11	Measurement: Time												✔
Summer Block 7	Week 12	Consolidation												

1   1 + 1 = ☐

1 mark

2   2 + 2 = ☐

1 mark

3   4 + 1 =

1 mark

4   6 + 3 =

1 mark

5 9 + 1 = ☐

1 mark

6 3 + 4 = ☐

1 mark

7 7 + 3 = ☐

1 mark

8 5 + 4 = ☐

1 mark

9   8 + 0 = ☐

1 mark

10   5 − 1 ☐

1 mark

Total marks ………/10

1 Complete the number track.

| 1 | 2 | | 4 | | 6 | 7 | | 9 | 10 |

2 Match the pictures to the correct numbers.
One has been done for you.

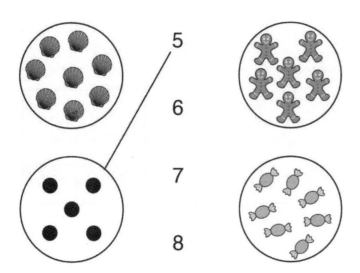

3 Draw the correct number of counters on each ten frame.

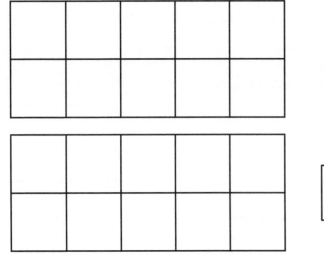

6

9

4

The arrow points to a number on the number line.
Tick the picture that represents that number.

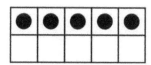   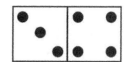

1 mark

5 Find **one more**.
One has been done for you.

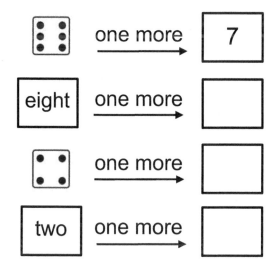

1 mark

6 I am one year **older** than my sister.
My sister is one year **older** than my brother.
My brother is 4.
How old am **I**?

years old

1 mark

7 Find **one less**.
One has been done for you.

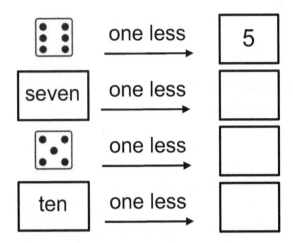

seven   one less ⟶ [ ]

one less ⟶ [ ]

ten   one less ⟶ [ ]

1 mark

8 Complete the table.

Picture	Number	Word
🐚🐚🐚🐚🐚		five
🧸🧸🧸🧸🧸🧸🧸🧸🧸	9	
🚗🚗🚗	3	

1 mark

9

Shakira put down **3** black counters.
Ben put down some **more**.
Complete the matching number sentence.

3 + [ ] = [ ]

1 mark

8

Name _____

10 Fill in the missing numbers.

| | 1 | 2 | | 4 | | 6 | | | 9 | |

11 Write a number in each box to make the sentences true.

is fewer than ☐.

is the same as ☐.

is more than ☐.

12 Complete the number track.

| one | two | | four | | six | seven | | nine | ten |

13 Joe has **4** marbles.
Erin has **fewer** marbles than Joe.
How many marbles could **Erin** have?

| marbles |

14

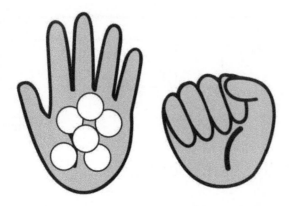

Sumi has 10 counters altogether in her hands.
She has 6 counters in one hand.
How many counters does she have in the other hand?

counters

1 mark

15 Tom has **6** stickers.
Raj has **fewer** stickers than Tom.
Alex has **more** stickers than Raj
but **fewer** stickers than Tom.
Who has the **most** stickers?

1 mark

Total marks ………/15

1   5 + 1 = ☐

1 mark

2   9 – 5 = ☐

1 mark

3 | 5 + 5 = [ ]

1 mark

4 | 3 + 5 = [ ]

1 mark

5 10 − 4 = ☐

1 mark

6 8 − 2 = ☐

1 mark

7   9 − 0 = ⬜

1 mark

8   8 = 7 + ⬜

1 mark

9 $2 +$ ☐ $= 9$

1 mark

10 $12 = 10 +$ ☐

1 mark

Total marks ………/10

1 Use these place value cards to make three different numbers between 10 and 20.

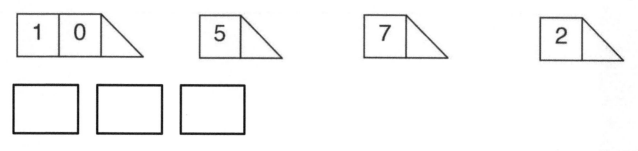

1 mark

2 Fill in the missing numbers on the number line.

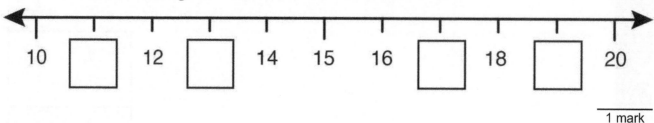

1 mark

3 Emily made a pattern with some beads.
Put a tick below her **fifth white bead**.

1 mark

4 Tick (✓) the names of the **two** shapes in this picture.

Tick (✓) **two**.

triangle ☐

square ☐

rectangle ☐

circle ☐

hexagon ☐

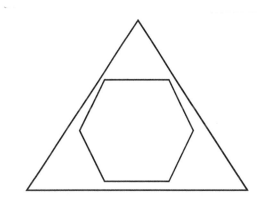

1 mark

5 There were **7** cars in the car park.
2 cars drove away.
How many cars are left in the car park?

	cars

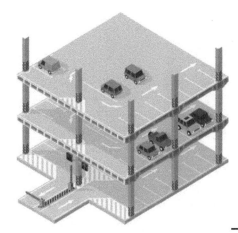

1 mark

6 Find one **more** or one **less**.
One has been done for you.

twelve	one **less** →	5

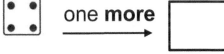 one **more** → ☐

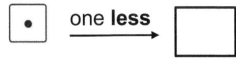 one **less** → ☐

twenty	one **less** →	☐

1 mark

7 Match each shape to its name.
One has been done for you.

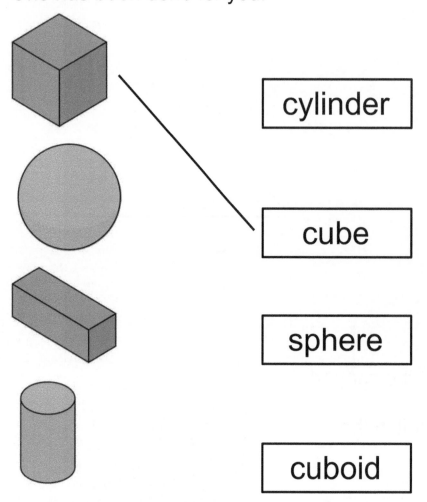

cylinder

cube

sphere

cuboid

____
1 mark

8 Complete the number track.

one	two	three	four	five	six	seven	eight	nine	ten
eleven	twelve	thirteen			sixteen		eighteen		twenty

____
1 mark

9 The arrow points to a number on the number line.

0   20

Tick (✓) the picture that represents that number.

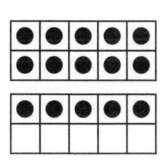

1 mark

10 Complete the part–whole model.

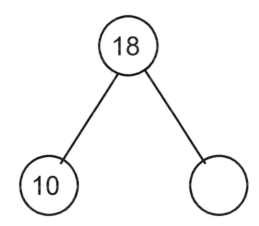

1 mark

11 My sister is **10**.
My brother is one year **older** than my sister.
I am one year **older** than my brother.
How old am **I**?

years old

1 mark

12 Leon put **8** black counters on the ten frame.
Then Sam took **5** counters off the ten frame.
Complete the matching number sentence.

$8 - \boxed{} = \boxed{}$

1 mark

13

Penalty Scoreboard	
Shakira	12
Emily	15
Tomas	11

The winner is the person who scored the **most** penalties.
Who came **second**?

1 mark

14 I am thinking of a number.
My number is **less than 16**.
My number is **greater than 14**.
What is my number?

1 mark

15 Tomas has **8** marbles.
Lucy has **more** marbles than Tomas.
Josef has less than **8** marbles.
Who has the **least** number of marbles?

1 mark

Total marks ………/15

1   6 + 4 = ☐

1 mark

2   9 − 3 = ☐

1 mark

3 [ ] = 5 + 5

1 mark

4 13 + 7 = [ ]

1 mark

23

5   12 + 7 = ☐

1 mark

6   11 − 7 = ☐

1 mark

7 30 + 8 =

1 mark

8 27 + 1 =

1 mark

9   49 − 9 = [   ]

1 mark

10   14 = 8 + [   ]

1 mark

11 $9 + \boxed{} = 12$

1 mark

12 $18 - \boxed{} = 7$

1 mark

Total marks ………/12

1 Put the numbers in order, from **smallest** to **largest**.

| 42 | 19 | 34 | 27 |

| | | | |

smallest   largest

1 mark

2 **Two** of these sentences are true.
Tick (✓) the true sentences.

1 less than 29 is 28.   1 more than 11 is 10.

1 more than 29 is 20.   1 fewer than 11 is 10.

1 mark

3 Sumi uses different shapes for tens and ones to make **16**.

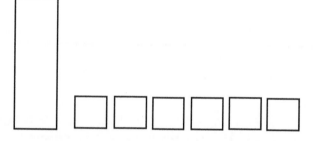

Sumi makes a new number below.

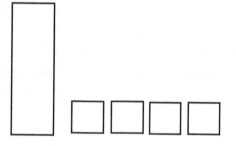

What is Sumi's new number?

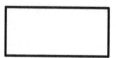

1 mark

28

4 Tick the **pyramid**.

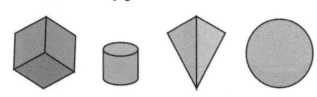

1 mark

5 Write the missing numbers.

| | is **1 less** than **30**. |

| | is **1 more** than **40**. |

1 mark

6 James had **17** marbles in his bag.
He took out **5** marbles to play a game.
How many marbles are in the bag now?

| marbles |

1 mark

7 On these cards, the word should match the number.
One of these cards is wrong.
Draw a cross (✘) on the card that is wrong.

| 13 | 9 | 7 | 5 |
| thirteen | nine | eleven | five |

1 mark

8 Draw lines to match the shapes to their names.

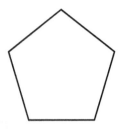

circle

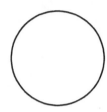

triangle

square

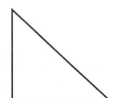

pentagon

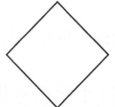

1 mark

9 Anna has the same number of buttons in each hand.
How many buttons does Anna have **altogether**?

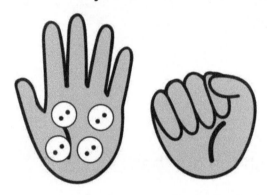

_____ buttons

1 mark

10 Fill in the missing numbers in the number sentences.

6 + ☐ = 9

16 + ☐ = 19

1 mark

11 Sanya has two small bunches of grapes in her lunch box.
One bunch has **11** grapes.
The other bunch has **7** grapes.
How many grapes does Sanya have **altogether**?

grapes

12

Put these digit cards together to make **two** different 2-digit numbers.
Write your numbers in order, beginning with the **smaller** number.

smaller   larger

13 Draw the next **two shapes** in this pattern.

14 Draw a ring around the odd one out.

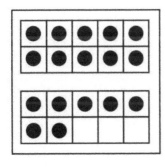   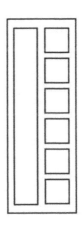   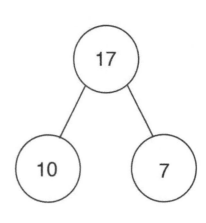

31

15 Fill in the missing numbers in the grid.

1	2	3	4	5	6	7	8	9	10
11	12	13		15	16	17	18	19	20
21	22				26		28	29	30
31	32	33		35	36		38	39	40
41	42	43	44	45	46				50

1 mark

16 Use **only** these numbers to write two subtraction number sentences.

| 8 | 17 | 9 |

☐ − ☐ = ☐

☐ − ☐ = ☐

1 mark

17 Mr Chen has **12** eggs.
He used **3** eggs to make a cake.
He used **6** eggs to make omelettes.
How many eggs are left?

12 eggs

☐ eggs

1 mark

18 Callum borrowed **3** books from the library.
Ellie borrowed **2 more** books than Callum.
How many books did Callum and
Ellie borrow **altogether**?

	books

1 mark

Total marks ..../18

1 2 + 2 = ⬚

1 mark

2 7 + 3 = ⬚

1 mark

3 | 8 – 7 = ☐

1 mark

4 | 17 – 3 = ☐

1 mark

5   34 − 1 = ☐

1 mark

6   10 + 10 = ☐

1 mark

7 36 − 6 = ☐

1 mark

8 29 − 1 = ☐

1 mark

9 40 + 4 = ☐

1 mark

10 19 − ☐ = 2

1 mark

11 18 = ☐ + 6

1 mark

12 11 + ☐ = 19

1 mark

Total marks ………/12

1 **Three** of these sentences are true.
  Tick (✓) the true sentences.

  1 less than 34 is 33.   1 more than 17 is 16.

  1 more than 49 is 50.   1 fewer than 30 is 29.

―――――
1 mark

2 Draw a **taller** tower.

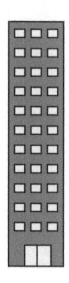

―――――
1 mark

3 Tick (✓) the hexagon.

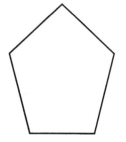 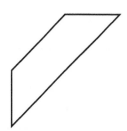 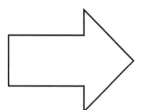 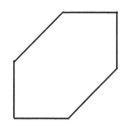

―――――
1 mark

4 Sam uses different shapes for tens and ones to make 34.

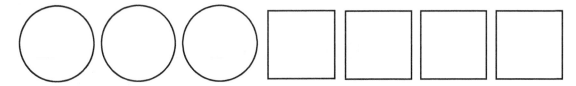

Sam makes a new number.

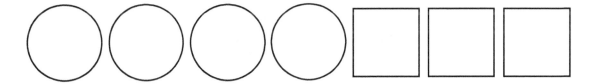

What is Sam's new number?

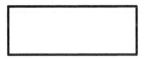

1 mark

5 Erin has **3** rings for the abacus.
She makes the number 3.

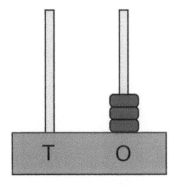

Which other numbers can she make, using **all** the rings?

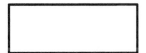

1 mark

6 Draw lines to match each shape to its name.

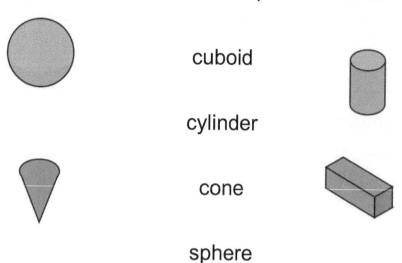

cuboid

cylinder

cone

sphere

7 Robin counted in **twos**.

Which **three** numbers did he say next?

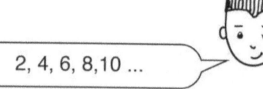

2, 4, 6, 8, 10 ...

☐ ☐ ☐

8 On these cards, the word should match the number.
One of these cards is wrong.
Draw a cross (✗) on the card that is wrong

19
nineteen

11
eleven

14
forty

12
twelve

9 **Tick** (✓) the shape that is heavier.

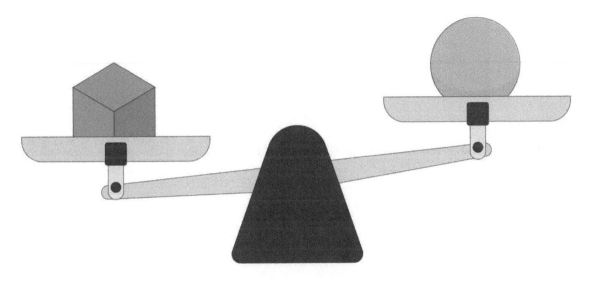

—————
1 mark

10 The numbers on this number line go up by the **same amount** each time.
Write the missing numbers in the boxes.

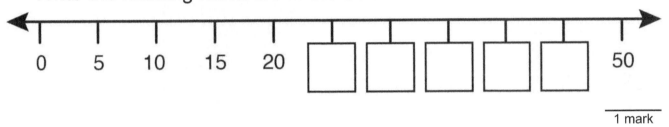

—————
1 mark

11 How long is the lizard?

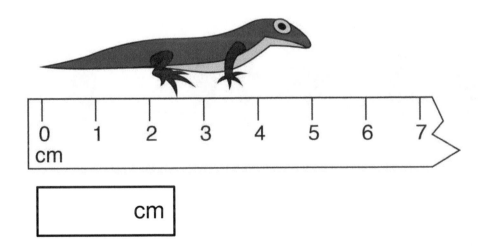

cm

—————
1 mark

12 Evan had a glass of milk.

Tick (✓) the glass that has **less** milk than Evan's.

13 Sumi had a pack of 50 felt pens.

She took out 10.
How many felt pens are in the pack now?

felt pens

50 pens

14 There were **7** birds resting on a wire.

9 more birds arrived.
How many birds are there now?

birds

15 Ellie counted in **twos** to find out how many socks she had.
How many socks are there **altogether**?

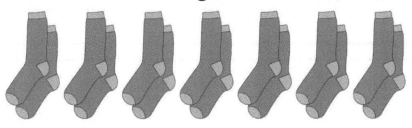

socks

1 mark

16 Make 6 different numbers, using two cards for each number.

Write your numbers in order, from smallest to largest.

smallest   largest

1 mark

17 Complete the number sentences.

$15 + 3 = \boxed{}$

$16 + \boxed{} = 19$

$\boxed{} + 3 = 20$

1 mark

18 One pan has 18 cubes in it.
The other pan has a toy car
and 5 cubes in it.
How many cubes weigh the
same as the toy car?

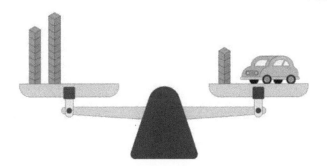

cubes

1 mark

Total marks ………/18

1 | 3 + 4 = ☐

1 mark

2 | 10 − 2 = ☐

1 mark

3   2 + 7 = ⬚

1 mark

4   17 + 3 = ⬚

1 mark

5 40 + 7 =

1 mark

6 2 + 2 + 2 =

1 mark

7 30 + 0 = ⬚

1 mark

8 $\frac{1}{2}$ of 10 = ⬚

1 mark

9 11 + 6 = ☐

1 mark

10 37 − 1 = ☐

1 mark

11 $44 - 4 = \boxed{}$

1 mark

12 $17 - \boxed{} = 5$

1 mark

13 $15 = \boxed{} + 9$

1 mark

14 $\frac{1}{4}$ of $4 = \boxed{}$

1 mark

15 | 9 + ☐ = 18

1 mark

Total marks ………/15

1 Put the four pencils in order, from **longest** to **shortest**.
One has been done for you.

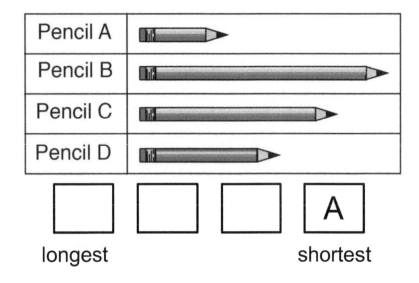

Pencil A	
Pencil B	
Pencil C	
Pencil D	

			A

longest   shortest

1 mark

2 Tick (✓) the **heavier** toy.

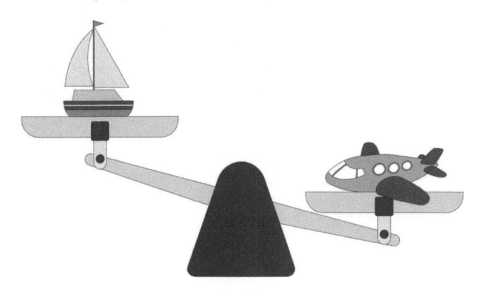

1 mark

3 Put the numbers in order, from **smallest** to **largest**.

43	49	37	26	31

smallest   largest

1 mark

4 Write the missing numbers.

1 mark

5 Match each abacus to its number.

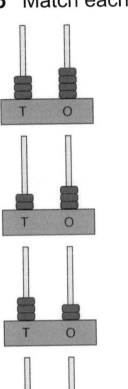

43

32

34

23

1 mark

6 Tick (✓) the names of the **two** shapes in this picture.

Tick (✓) **two**.

cube ☐

cuboid ☐

sphere ☐

pyramid ☐

cylinder ☐

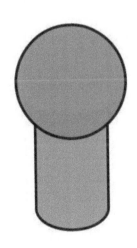

1 mark

7

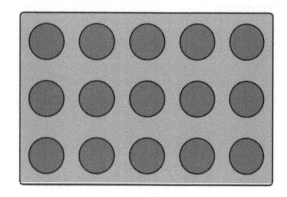

How many circles in each **row**?   ☐

How many circles in each **column**?   ☐

How many circles **altogether**?   ☐

8 Start at the triangle.
Move **2** squares up.
Move **1** square right.
Draw a circle in that square.

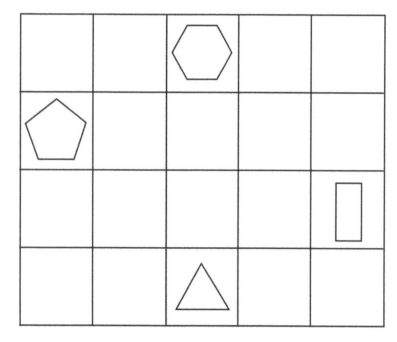

9 Tick (✓) the shapes that show **half**.

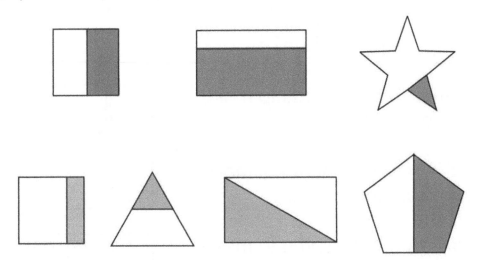

1 mark

10 How many spots are there on a double **6** domino?

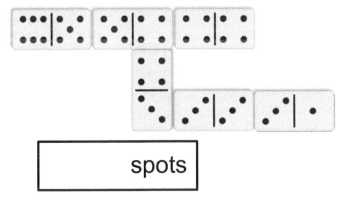

spots

1 mark

11 Tom is facing the flowers.
Tom turns **three-quarters** of a turn clockwise.
Tick (✓) the object Tom is facing now.

1 mark

12

| 2 | 3 | 4 |

Use two **different** digit cards to make a number greater than 40.

Use two **different** digit cards to make the smallest number you can.

Use two **different** digit cards to make a number less than 30.

1 mark

13 Sarah has **8** shells.
Jonah has **5** more shells than Sarah.
How many shells does **Jonah** have?

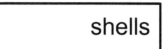

1 mark

14 Fill in the missing numbers.

| 2 | 0 | + | 8 | = | | |

| | | + | 2 | = | 3 | 2 |

| 4 | 0 | + | | = | 4 | 7 |

1 mark

15 Tick (✓) the glass that is **half full**.

1 mark

16 Bonnie has **19** counters altogether
in her hands.
She has **6** in one hand.
How many counters are there
in her other hand?

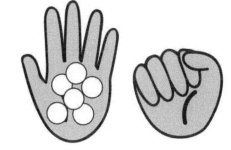

counters

1 mark

17 The car park is full.
There are **4** rows of cars in the car park.
Each row has **5** cars in it.
How many cars are in the car park?

cars

1 mark

18 Will had **9** marbles.
After Will won some marbles,
he had **13** marbles **altogether**.
How many marbles did Will win?

marbles

1 mark

19 Mum bought Tanya a pack
of **12** socks.
How many **pairs** of socks
can Tanya make?

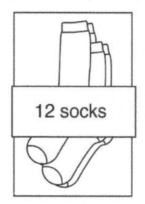

12 socks

pairs of socks

1 mark

20 Elena has one more sticker than Gemma.
They have **15** stickers altogether.
How many stickers does **Elena** have?

stickers

1 mark

Total marks ………/20

1   5 + 3 = ⬜

1 mark

2   9 – 5 = ⬜

1 mark

3   17 + 1 = ☐

1 mark

4   14 + 0 = ☐

1 mark

5 5 + 5 + 5 = ☐

1 mark

6 90 + 2 = ☐

1 mark

7 67 − 1 = ☐

1 mark

8 86 − 6 = ☐

1 mark

9 73 + 1 = ☐

1 mark

10 $\frac{1}{2}$ of 20 = ☐

1 mark

11 12 + 7 = ☐

1 mark

12 $\frac{1}{4}$ of 8 = ☐

1 mark

13 $19 - \boxed{} = 4$

1 mark

14 $\boxed{} - 9 = 8$

1 mark

15 7 + ☐ = 16

1 mark

Total marks ………/15

1   Each number has been split into tens and ones.
    Complete the part–whole diagrams.

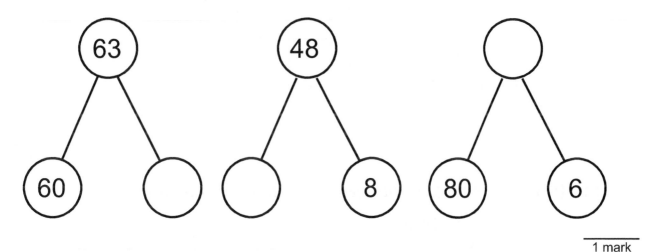

1 mark

2   Put each number into the machine.
    What numbers will come out of the machine?

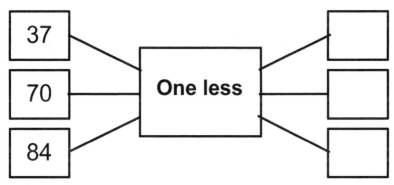

1 mark

3   Finn left home at **8 o'clock.**
    Tick (✓) the clock that shows 8 o'clock.

1 mark

Name _____

4 Put the numbers in order, from **smallest** to **largest**.

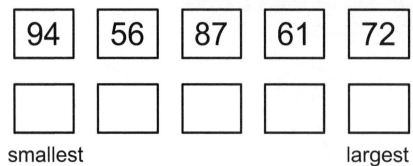

| 94 | 56 | 87 | 61 | 72 |

smallest   largest

1 mark

5 **Tick (✓)** the names of the **two** shapes in this picture.

Tick (✓) **two**.

circle ☐

triangle ☐

square ☐

rectangle ☐

pentagon ☐

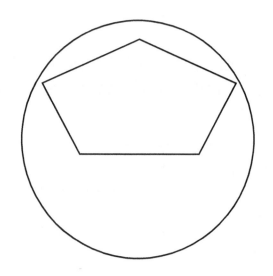

1 mark

6 What time does the clock show?
Tick (✓) the correct box.

| half past 4 | | three o'clock |

| half past 3 | | half past 2 |

1 mark

7 Ivy has **eight** 2p coins.
How much money does Ivy have **altogether**?

p

8 How long is the snake?

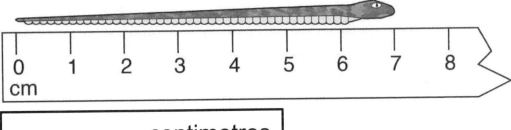

centimetres

9 Complete these pieces from
the 100 square.

57		59
	68	
77		79

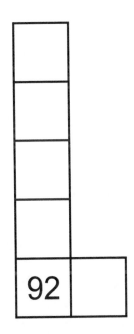

10 Fill in the missing numbers.

1 mark

11 These are the items in the school chest of drawers.

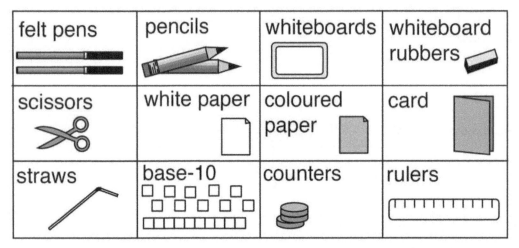

What is in the third drawer from the left in the top row?

What is in the second drawer from the right in the bottom row?

1 mark

12 Ella has seven £10 notes.
How much money does Ella have?

£

1 mark

13 Today is Friday.

What day was it yesterday? _____

What day will it be tomorrow? _____

14 Luke made some ice cubes.

How many ice cubes are in each **row**? ☐

How many ice cubes are in each **column**? ☐

How many ice cubes are there **altogether**? ☐

15 Alfie has **9** grapes.
Ezra has **double** the amount Alfie has.
How many grapes does **Ezra** have?

_____ grapes

16 There were **17** balls in the bag.
Heidi took out **12** balls.
How many balls are in the bag now?

balls

17 How much is **half** this amount of money?

p

18 Order the toys, from **lightest** to **heaviest**.

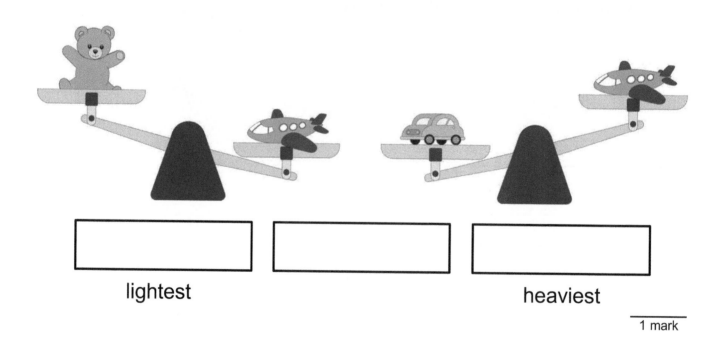

lightest		heaviest

19 There are **20** flowers.
Mum puts **5** flowers in each vase.
How many vases does she
need for all the flowers?

vases

1 mark

20 Tick the fraction that is shaded in this shape.

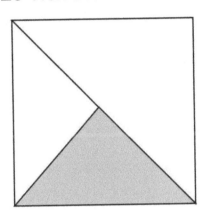

$\dfrac{1}{2}$ $\dfrac{1}{4}$

1 mark

Total marks ..../20

Year 1 Autumn Half Term 1: Arithmetic Mark Scheme

Question	Requirement	Mark	Level of demand
1	2	1	T
2	4	1	T
3	5	1	T
4	9	1	E
5	10	1	E
6	7	1	E
7	10	1	E
8	9	1	E
9	8	1	G
10	4	1	G

Threshold scores
Working towards the expected standard (T): 5 or fewer
Working at the expected standard (E): 6–7
Working at greater depth (G): 8–10

Balance of difficulty of questions in the paper
3 marks at working towards (T)
5 marks at the expected standard (E)
2 marks at working at greater depth (G)

Year 1 Autumn Half Term 1: Reasoning Mark Scheme

Question	Requirement	Mark	Additional guidance	Level of demand
1	Completed number track. 1 2 3 4 5 6 7 8 9 10	1	All numbers must be in the correct space for the award of the mark. Accept any other clear way of indicating the correct answer, e.g. writing the number above or below the relevant space.	T
2	Pictures and numbers matched as shown.	1	All three numbers must be correctly matched for award of the mark.	T
3	Ten frames completed as shown.	1	Both ten frames must contain the correct number of counters for award of the mark. Accept counters placed in any space within the ten frame, provided there is a single counter in any one space.	T
4	Representation of 6 ticked as shown.	1	Accept any other clear way of indicating the correct answer e.g crossed out representations of 5 and 7.	E
5	Numbers completed as shown. [dice 6] one more → 7 eight one more → 9 [dice 4] one more → 5 two one more → 3	1	All three numbers must be correctly completed for award of the mark.	E
6	6 (years old)	1		E
7	Numbers completed as shown. [dice 6] one less → 5 seven one less → 6 [dice 5] one less → 4 ten one less → 9	1	All three numbers must be correctly completed for award of the mark.	E
8	Table completed as shown. 	Picture	Number	Word	 |---|---|---| 	●●●●●	**5**	five	 	[bears]	9	**nine**	 	[cars]	3	**three**		1	All three numbers or words must be correctly completed for award of the mark. Accept misspellings of number words provided the intention is clear.	E

9	Number sentence completed as shown. $3 +$ 5 $=$ 8	1	Both numbers must be correctly completed for award of the mark.	E
10	Number line completed as shown. 0 1 2 3 4 5 6 7 8 9 10	1	All numbers must be in the correct order for the award of the mark. Accept any other clear way of indicating the correct answer, e.g. writing the number above or below the appropriate place on the number line.	E
11	(bananas) is fewer than 10 . (bananas) is the same as 7 . (bananas) is more than 1 .	1	All three numbers must be correct for the award of the mark. Accept any number greater than 10 in the first box. Accept 0 in the last box.	E
12	Number track completed as shown: one | two | **three** | four | **five** | six | seven | **eight** | nine | ten	1	All three number words must be correctly completed for award of the mark. Accept misspellings of number words provided the intention is clear.	E
13	1, 2 or 3	1	A single correct number is sufficient for the award of the mark. Accept any or all of the three possible answers. **Do not** accept 0 as an answer.	G
14	4 (counters)	1		G
15	Tom	1		G

Threshold scores
Working towards the expected standard (T): 8 or fewer
Working at the expected standard (E): 9–11
Working at greater depth (G): 12–15

Balance of difficulty of questions in the paper
3 marks at working towards (T)
9 marks at the expected standard (E)
3 marks at working at greater depth (G)

Year 1 Autumn Half Term 2: Arithmetic Mark Scheme

Question	Requirement	Mark	Level of demand
1	6	1	T
2	4	1	T
3	10	1	T
4	8	1	E
5	6	1	E
6	6	1	E
7	9	1	E
8	1	1	G
9	7	1	G
10	2	1	G

Threshold scores
Working towards the expected standard (T): 5 or fewer
Working at the expected standard (E): 6–7
Working at greater depth (G): 8–10

Balance of difficulty of questions in the paper
3 marks at working towards (T)
4 marks at the expected standard (E)
3 marks at working at greater depth (G)

Year 1 Autumn Half Term 2: Reasoning Mark Scheme

Question	Requirement	Mark	Additional guidance	Level of demand
1	Numbers as shown. `12` `15` `17`	1	All three numbers must be correct for the award of the mark. Accept the numbers in any order.	T
2	Number line completed as shown. 10 `11` 12 `13` 14 15 16 `17` 18 `19` 20	1	All four numbers must be correct for award of the mark. Accept any other way of recording the numbers, provided the intention is clear.	T
3	Fifth white bead ticked as shown. ○○●●○●●●○○●● ✔	1	Accept any other way of indicating the correct bead.	T
4	Two shape names ticked as shown. triangle ✔ square ☐ rectangle ☐ circle ☐ hexagon ✔	1	Both names must be correctly ticked for award of the mark. Accept any other clear way of indicating the correct answer, e.g names ringed.	E
5	5 (cars)	1		E
6	twelve — one **less** → 5 [4 dots] — one **more** → 5 [1 dot] — one **less** → 0 twenty — one **less** → 19	1	All three numbers must be correct for the award of the mark.	E
7	3D shapes and names matched as indicated: cylinder cube sphere cuboid	1	All three shapes and names must be correctly matched for the award of the mark. Accept any other way of linking shapes and names, provided the intention is clear.	E
8	Number track completed as shown.			E

one	two	three	four	five	six	seven	eight	nine	ten
eleven	twelve	thirteen	**fourteen**	**fifteen**	sixteen	**seventeen**	eighteen	**nineteen**	twenty

		Mark	Additional guidance	
		1	All four number words must be correctly completed for award of the mark. Accept misspellings of number words provided the intention is clear.	

Year 1 Autumn Half Term 2: Reasoning Mark Scheme

9	The matching representation for 13 ticked.	1	Accept other methods of highlighting the correct representation, provided the intention is clear.	E
10	Part–whole model completed as shown:	1	Accept other ways of recording the correct answer, e.g. number written outside the part circle.	E
11	12 (years old)	1		E
12	Number sentence completed as shown. $8 - \boxed{5} = \boxed{3}$	1	Both numbers must be correct for award of the mark. Do not accept representations such as the crossing out of 5 counters unless the number sentence is also completed.	E
13	Shakira	1	Accept other indication of the correct answer e.g. a ring around the name Shakira.	G
14	15	1		G
15	Josef	1		G

Threshold scores
Working towards the expected standard (T): 8 or fewer
Working at the expected standard (E): 9–11
Working at greater depth (G): 12–15

Balance of difficulty of questions in the paper
3 marks at working towards (T)
9 marks at the expected standard (E)
3 marks at working at greater depth (G)

Year 1 Spring Half Term 1: Arithmetic Mark Scheme

Question	Requirement	Mark	Level of demand
1	10	1	T
2	6	1	T
3	10	1	T
4	20	1	E
5	19	1	E
6	4	1	E
7	38	1	E
8	28	1	E
9	40	1	E
10	6	1	G
11	3	1	G
12	11	1	G

Threshold scores
Working towards the expected standard (T): 6 or fewer
Working at the expected standard (E): 7–9
Working at greater depth (G): 10–12

Balance of difficulty of questions in the paper
3 marks at working towards (T)
6 marks at the expected standard (E)
3 marks at working at greater depth (G)

Year 1 Spring Half Term 1: Reasoning Mark Scheme

Question	Requirement	Mark	Additional guidance	Level of demand
1	Numbers in order as shown. 19 27 34 42 smallest largest	1	All four numbers must be in the correct order for the award of the mark. Accept other ways of indicating the order, e.g. a line drawn from each number to its correct place in the ordered list.	T
2	Sentences as shown. 1 less than 29 is 28. ✓ 1 more than 11 is 10. 1 more than 29 is 20. 1 fewer than 11 is 10. ✓	1	Both correct number sentences must be ticked for award of the mark. Accept any other way of indicating the correct sentences, e.g. crossing out the incorrect sentences.	T
3	14	1	Do not accept 10 + 4 unless the total 14 is provided.	T
4		1	Accept any other clear way of indicating the pyramid.	E
5	☐ is **1 less** than. **30**. ☐ is **1 more** than **40**.	1	Both numbers must be correctly completed for award of the mark.	E
6	12 (marbles)	1		E
7		1	Accept any other way of indicating the correct answer, provided the intention is clear.	E
8		1	Each of the four shapes must be correctly linked to its name for award of the mark.	E
9	8 (buttons)	1		E
10	Number sentences completed as shown. 6 + [3] = 9 16 + [3] = 19	1	Both number sentences must be correctly completed for award of the mark.	E
11	18 (grapes)	1		E
12	Numbers ordered as shown. 24 42 smaller larger	1	Both numbers must be correct for award of the mark.	E
13		1	Both shapes must be correctly added for award of the mark. Accept slight inaccuracies in drawings provided the intention is clear.	E

14	Middle box ringed as shown. 	1	Accept other ways of indicating the correct answer, e.g. ticking the middle box or ticking the other two boxes, provided the intention is clear.	E
15	Grid completed as shown. <table><tr><td>1</td><td>2</td><td>3</td><td>4</td><td>5</td><td>6</td><td>7</td><td>8</td><td>9</td><td>10</td></tr><tr><td>11</td><td>12</td><td>13</td><td>**14**</td><td>15</td><td>16</td><td>17</td><td>18</td><td>19</td><td>20</td></tr><tr><td>21</td><td>22</td><td>**23**</td><td>**24**</td><td>**25**</td><td>26</td><td>**27**</td><td>28</td><td>29</td><td>30</td></tr><tr><td>31</td><td>32</td><td>33</td><td>**34**</td><td>35</td><td>36</td><td>**37**</td><td>38</td><td>39</td><td>40</td></tr><tr><td>41</td><td>42</td><td>43</td><td>44</td><td>45</td><td>46</td><td>**47**</td><td>**48**</td><td>**49**</td><td>50</td></tr></table>	1	All the missing numbers must be correctly completed for award of the mark.	E
16	Use only these numbers to write two subtraction number sentences. $$17 - 8 = 9$$ $$17 - 9 = 8$$	1	Both number sentences must be correctly completed for award of the mark. Accept the number sentences in any order. Do not accept the sentences if numbers other than those given in the question have been used.	G
17	3 (eggs)	1		G
18	8 (books)	1		G

Threshold scores
Working towards the expected standard (T): 9 or fewer
Working at the expected standard (E): 10–14
Working at greater depth (G): 15–18

Balance of difficulty of questions in the paper
3 marks at working towards (T)
12 marks at the expected standard (E)
3 marks at working at greater depth (G)

Year 1 Spring Half Term 2: Arithmetic Mark Scheme

Question	Requirement	Mark	Level of demand
1	4	1	T
2	10	1	T
3	1	1	T
4	14	1	E
5	33	1	E
6	20	1	E
7	30	1	E
8	28	1	E
9	44	1	E
10	17	1	G
11	12	1	G
12	8	1	G

Threshold scores
Working towards the expected standard (T): 6 or fewer
Working at the expected standard (E): 7–9
Working at greater depth (G): 10–12

Balance of difficulty of questions in the paper
3 marks at working towards (T)
6 marks at the expected standard (E)
3 marks at working at greater depth (G)

Year 1 Spring Half Term 2: Reasoning Mark Scheme

Question	Requirement	Mark	Additional guidance	Level of demand
1	1 less than 34 is 33. ✔ 1 more than 17 is 16. 1 more than 49 is 50. ✔ 1 fewer than 30 is 29. ✔	1	All three correct statements must be ticked for the award of the mark. Accept other ways of indicating which statements are correct, e.g. crossing out the incorrect statement, provided the intention is clear.	T
2	Any tower that is clearly taller than the given tower.	1	Accept any tower that is clearly taller than the given tower.	T
3	Hexagon ticked as shown. 	1	Accept any other way of indicating which shape is the hexagon, e.g. a ring around it.	T
4	43	1		E
5	12, 21, 30	1	All three numbers must be correct for award of the mark. Accept the numbers in any order, ignoring any duplicates provided all three numbers are given.	E
6	Lines drawn to match shapes to names. 	1	All four shapes must be correctly linked to their names for award of the mark.	E
7	Next three numbers are: 	1	All three numbers must be correct, and in the correct order, for award of the mark.	E
8		1	Accept other ways of indicating the correct answer, e.g. the correct cards ticked, provided the intention is clear.	E
9	The cube is heavier. 	1	Accept any other way of indicating that the cube is heavier, provided the intention is clear.	E
10	Number line completed as shown. 	1	All missing numbers must be correctly completed for award of the mark.	E
11	5 (centimetres)	1		E
12	Third glass ticked as indicated. 	1	Accept any other way of indicating the correct glass, provided the intention is clear.	E
13	40 (felt pens)	1		E

Year 1 Spring Half Term 2: Reasoning Mark Scheme

14	16 (birds)	1		E
15	14 (socks)	1		E
16	Numbers ordered as below. 23 24 32 34 42 43 smallest largest	1	All six numbers must be correctly completed and ordered for award of the mark. Do not award the mark if the numbers have not been recorded in the correct order.	G
17	Number sentences completed as shown. $15 + 3 = \boxed{18}$ $16 + \boxed{3} = 19$ $\boxed{17} + 3 = 20$	1	All three sentences must be correctly completed for award of the mark.	G
18	13 (cubes)	1		G

Threshold scores
Working towards the expected standard (T): 9 or fewer
Working at the expected standard (E): 10–14
Working at greater depth (G): 15–18

Balance of difficulty of questions in the paper
3 marks at working towards (T)
12 marks at the expected standard (E)
3 marks at working at greater depth (G)

Year 1 Summer Half Term 1: Arithmetic Mark Scheme

Question	Requirement	Mark	Level of demand
1	7	1	T
2	8	1	T
3	9	1	T
4	20	1	T
5	47	1	E
6	6	1	E
7	30	1	E
8	5	1	E
9	17	1	E
10	36	1	E
11	40	1	E
12	12	1	G
13	6	1	G
14	1	1	G
15	9	1	G

Threshold scores
Working towards the expected standard (T): 8 or fewer
Working at the expected standard (E): 9–11
Working at greater depth (G): 12–15

Balance of difficulty of questions in the paper
4 marks at working towards (T)
7 marks at the expected standard (E)
4 marks at working at greater depth (G)

Year 1 Summer Half Term 1: Reasoning Mark Scheme

Question	Requirement	Mark	Additional guidance	Level of demand
1	B C D A longest — shortest	1	All three letters must be in the correct order for award of the mark. Accept any other way of showing the order, provided the intention is clear.	T
2	Toy aeroplane ticked as shown. 	1	Accept any other way of indicating the aeroplane is heavier, provided the intention is clear.	T
3	Numbers ordered as shown. 26 31 37 43 49 smallest — largest	1	Accept reverse order provided the labels smallest and largest have been swapped.	T
4	Numbers completed as shown. 5 — 5 less — 10 — 5 more — 15	1	Both numbers must be correctly completed for the award of the mark.	T
5	Abacus and number matched as shown. 	1	All four abaci and numbers must be correctly matched for award of the mark. Accept any other method of matching, provided the intention is clear.	E
6	Two shapes ticked as shown. cube ☐ cuboid ☐ sphere ✓ pyramid ☐ cylinder ✓	1	Both shapes must be ticked for award of the mark. Accept other methods of indicating the two shapes, e.g. drawing a ring around each of the two required names.	E
7	Boxes completed as shown. How many circles in each **row**? 5 How many circles in each **column**? 3 How many circles **altogether**? 15	1	All three numbers must be correct for award of the mark.	E

Year 1 Summer Half Term 1: Reasoning Mark Scheme

8	Grid completed with circle in the second row, 4 squares from the left.	1	The circle must be in the correct square for award of the mark.	E
9	Shapes ticked as below.	1	All three shapes which show halves must be ticked for award of the mark. Do not award the mark if other shapes are ticked, unless the intention is clear.	E
10	12 (spots)	1		E
11	Tom will be facing the bookshelves.	1	Accept any other way of indicating which way Tom is facing, provided the intention is clear.	E
12	Numbers completed as shown. Two different digit cards used to make a number greater than 40. $\boxed{4}\,\boxed{2}$ OR $\boxed{4}\,\boxed{3}$ Two different digit cards used to make the smallest possible number. $\boxed{2}\,\boxed{3}$ Two different digit cards used to make a number less than 30. $\boxed{2}\,\boxed{3}$ OR $\boxed{2}\,\boxed{4}$	1	All three numbers must be correct for the award of the mark.	E
13	13 (shells)	1		E
14	Numbers completed as shown. $\boxed{2}\,\boxed{0} + \boxed{8} = \boxed{2}\,\boxed{8}$ $\boxed{3}\,\boxed{0} + \boxed{2} = \boxed{3}\,\boxed{2}$ $\boxed{4}\,\boxed{0} + \boxed{7} = \boxed{4}\,\boxed{7}$	1	All three numbers must be correctly completed for award of the mark.	E
15	Fourth glass ticked as shown.	1	Accept other ways of indicating the appropriate glass, e.g. drawing a ring around it, provided the intention is clear.	E

Year 1 Summer Half Term 1: Reasoning Mark Scheme

16	13 (counters)	1		E
17	20 (cars)	1		G
18	4 (marbles)	1		G
19	6 (pairs of socks)	1		G
20	8 (stickers)	1		G

Threshold scores
Working towards the expected standard (T): 11 or fewer
Working at the expected standard (E): 12–15
Working at greater depth (G): 16–20

Balance of difficulty of questions in the paper
4 marks at working towards (T)
12 marks at the expected standard (E)
4 marks at working at greater depth (G)

Year 1 Summer Half Term 2: Arithmetic Mark Scheme

Question	Requirement	Mark	Level of demand
1	8	1	T
2	4	1	T
3	18	1	T
4	14	1	E
5	15	1	E
6	92	1	E
7	66	1	E
8	80	1	E
9	74	1	E
10	10	1	E
11	19	1	E
12	2	1	G
13	15	1	G
14	17	1	G
15	9	1	G

Threshold scores
Working towards the expected standard (T): 8 or fewer
Working at the expected standard (E): 9–11
Working at greater depth (G): 12–15

Balance of difficulty of questions in the paper
3 marks at working towards (T)
8 marks at the expected standard (E)
4 marks at working at greater depth (G)

Year 1 Summer Half Term 2: Reasoning Mark Scheme

Question	Requirement	Mark	Additional guidance	Level of demand
1	Part–whole diagrams completed as shown. 63 → 60, 3 48 → 40, 8 86 → 80, 6	1	All three part–whole diagrams must be correctly completed for award of the mark.	T
2	Machine output completed as shown. 37 → 36 70 → 69 "One less" 84 → 83	1	All three output numbers must be correctly completed for award of the mark. Accept the outputs completed in any order, provided all three numbers are correct.	T
3	8 o'clock ticked. 	1	Accept other ways of indicating the correct clock, provided the intention is clear.	T
4	Numbers ordered as shown. 56 61 72 87 94 smallest largest	1	Accept numbers in reverse order provided the labels have also been changed.	T
5	Circle and pentagon ticked. circle ✓ triangle square rectangle pentagon ✓	1	Both shapes must be indicated for award of the mark. Accept other ways of indicating the shapes, e.g. ringing the relevant names.	E
6	Half past 3 ticked. half past 4 three o'clock half past 3 ✓ half past 2	1	Accept other ways of indicating the correct time.	E
7	16 (p)	1		E
8	7 (centimetres)	1		E
9	52 62 72 82 92 93 57 58 59 67 68 69 77 78 79	1	All numbers must be correctly completed for award of the mark.	E

Year 1 Summer Half Term 2: Reasoning Mark Scheme

10	Numbers completed as shown. `60` ←10 less `70` 10 more→ `80`	1	Both numbers must be correct for the award of the mark.	E
11	Third drawer from the left in the top row whiteboards Second drawer from the right in the bottom row counters	1	Both answers must be correct for award of the mark. Accept variations in spelling, provided the intention is clear.	E
12	(£) 70	1		E
13	Yesterday Thursday Tomorrow Saturday	1	Both answers must be correct for award of the mark. Accept variations in spelling, provided the intention is clear.	E
14	How many ice cubes in each **row**? `10` How many ice cubes in each **column**? `2` How many ice cubes **altogether**? `20`	1	All three answers must be correct for award of the mark.	E
15	18 (grapes)	1		E
16	5 (balls)	1		E
17	7 (p)	1		G
18	Toys ordered as shown. `teddy bear` `aeroplane` `car` lightest heaviest	1	Accept other ways of indicating the correct toys, e.g. arrows to their order position, drawing in the boxes etc, provided the intention is clear.	G
19	4 (vases)	1		G
20	¼ ticked. $\frac{1}{2}$ $\frac{1}{4}$ ✔	1		G

Threshold scores
Working towards the expected standard (T): 11 or fewer
Working at the expected standard (E): 12–15
Working at greater depth (G): 16–20

Balance of difficulty of questions in the paper
4 marks at working towards (T)
12 marks at the expected standard (E)
4 marks at working at greater depth (G)

Content domain references

Autumn 1: Arithmetic	
Question	**Content domain reference**
1	1N2b/1C1
2	1N1b/1C1
3	1N2b/1C1
4	1C2b/1C1
5	1N2b/1C1
6	1C2b/1C1
7	1C2b/1C1
8	1C2b/1C1
9	1C2b/1C1
10	1N2b/1C1

Autumn 2: Arithmetic	
Question	**Content domain reference**
1	1N2b/1C2b
2	1C2a/1C2b
3	1N1b/1C2b
4	1C2a/1C2b
5	1C2a/1C2b
6	1C2a/1C2b
7	1C2a/1C2b
8	1C4/1C2b
9	1C4/1C2b
10	1C4/1C2b

Autumn 1: Reasoning	
Question	**Content domain reference**
1	1N1a/1N2a
2	1N2a/1N2c
3	1N2a/1N4
4	1N1a/1N4
5	1N2b
6	1N2b/1C2a
7	1N2b
8	1N2c
9	1C1/1C2b
10	1N1a/1N2c
11	1N4/1N2b
12	1N2c
13	1N4/1C4
14	1C2a/1C4
15	1N4/1C4

Autumn 2: Reasoning	
Question	**Content domain reference**
1	1N2c
2	1N2a/1N2b
3	1N4
4	1G1a
5	1C4/1C1
6	1N2b
7	1G1b
8	1N2c
9	1N1a/1N4
10	1N4/1C1
11	1N2b/1C4
12	1C2b/1C1
13	1N4/1C4
14	1N4/1C4
15	1N4/1C1

Content domain references

Spring 1: Arithmetic	
Question	Content domain reference
1	1C2a/1C1
2	1C2a/1C1
3	1N1b/1C1
4	1C2a/1C1
5	1N1b/1C1
6	1N1b/1C1
7	1C2b/1C4
8	1N2b/1C4
9	1C2b/1C4
10	1C4/1C2b
11	1C4/1C2b
12	1C4/1C2b

Spring 2: Arithmetic	
Question	Content domain reference
1	1N1b/1C1
2	1C2a/1C1
3	1C2a/1C1
4	1C2a/1C1
5	1N2b/1C1
6	1N1b/1C1
7	1C2b/1C4
8	1N2b/1C4
9	1C2b/1C4
10	1C4/1C2b
11	1C4/1C2b
12	1C4/1C2b

Spring 1: Reasoning	
Question	Content domain reference
1	1N2a/1N1a
2	1N2b/1N4
3	1N4
4	1G1b
5	1N2b/1N4
6	1C2a/1C4
7	1N2c
8	1G1a
9	1C2a/1C4
10	1C1/1C2b
11	1C2a/1C4
12	1N2a
13	1G1a/1P2
14	1N4
15	1N1a/1N2b
16	1C2b/1C4
17	1C2a/1C4
18	1C2a/1C4

Spring 2: Reasoning	
Question	Content domain reference
1	1N2b
2	1M1
3	1G1a
4	1N4
5	1N2a/1N4
6	1G1b
7	1N1b/1N2c
8	1N2c
9	1M1
10	1N1b
11	1M2
12	1M1
13	1C4/1N2a
14	1C4/1N2a
15	1N1b
16	1N2a
17	1C2b/1C4
18	1M1/1M2

Content domain references

Summer 1: Arithmetic	
Question	**Content domain reference**
1	1C1/1C2a
2	1C1/1C2a
3	1C1/1C2a
4	1C1/1C2a
5	1C2b/1N2a
6	1N1b
7	1C2b/1N2a
8	1F1a
9	1C1/1C2a
10	1N2b
11	1C2b/1N2a
12	1C2b/1C4
13	1C2b/1C4
14	1F1b
15	1C2b/1C4

Summer 2: Arithmetic	
Question	**Content domain reference**
1	1C1/1C2a
2	1C1/1C2a
3	1N2b
4	1C1/1C2a
5	1N1b
6	1C2b/1N2a
7	1N2b
8	1C2b/1N2a
9	1C1/1C2a
10	1F1a
11	1C2b/1N2a
12	1F1b
13	1C2b/1C4
14	1C2b/1C4
15	1C2b/1C4

Summer 1: Reasoning	
Question	**Content domain reference**
1	1M1
2	1M1
3	1N2a
4	1N1b
5	1N4
6	1G1b
7	1C8
8	1P2
9	1G1a
10	1C2a/1C4
11	1P2
12	1N2a
13	1C2a/1C4
14	1N2a
15	1M1
16	1C2a/1C4
17	1N1b/1C8
18	1C2a/1C4
19	1N1b/1C8
20	1N4/1C4

Summer 2: Reasoning	
Question	**Content domain reference**
1	1N2a/1N4
2	1N2b
3	1M4a
4	1N2a/1N4
5	1G1a
6	1M4a
7	1N1b/1M3
8	1M2
9	1N1b/1N2b
10	1N1b/1N2a
11	1P2
12	1N1b/1M3
13	1M4b/1M4c
14	1C8/1N1b
15	1C8
16	1C2a
17	1F1a
18	1M1
19	1C8
20	1F1b

Name _____   Class _____

Year 1/P2 Maths Progress Tests for White Rose Record Sheet

Tests	Mark	Total marks	Key skills to target
Autumn 1: Arithmetic			
Autumn 1: Reasoning			
Autumn 2: Arithmetic			
Autumn 2: Reasoning			
Spring 1: Arithmetic			
Spring 1: Reasoning			
Spring 2: Arithmetic			
Spring 2: Reasoning			
Summer 1: Arithmetic			
Summer 1: Reasoning			
Summer 2: Arithmetic			
Summer 2: Reasoning			